Participant Guide:

Teambuilding, Leadership, Diversity & Sexual Harassment

Caroline Wee

DEDICATION

To my beloved Kelly. I am eternally grateful for the love, support, and
encouragement you have shown me every single day. Thank you for truly believing I
can change the world. You have certainly changed mine!

CONTENTS

Introduction

1   Teamwork   Pg. 8

2   Leadership   Pg. 19

3   Diversity   Pg. 44

4   Sexual Harassment Pg. 60

10 About the Author Pg. 76

INTRODUCATION

This workbook is designed to provide a convenient and cost effective solution for participants of the Wee Communicate Trainings on Teambuilding, Leadership, Diversity and Sexual Harassment. This guide contains all of the documents necessary for participants to complete these trainings.

1 TEAMWORK

"None of us is as smart as all of us." ~ Ken Blanchard

Full Training Agenda

➤ **Section One: Getting Started**
- Agenda
- Introduction & Biography
- Objectives
- Icebreaker
- Benefits of a Diverse Team
- Elements of Teamwork
- Team Roles
- Review

➤ **Section Two: Team Alignment**
- Personalities
- Gender Communications
- Assignment
- Review

Icebreaker Interview Slips

Interview Questions:

1. What is your name?

2. What is your position within the company?

3. How long have you been with the company?

4. What is your favorite thing about working for the company?

5. What is your favorite thing to do in your free time?

Elements of Teamwork

- Communication

- Interpersonal Relations

- Optimum task delegation

- Aligned goals

- Motivation

- Commitment

- Trust

- Diversity

- Creativity

- Collaboration

- Conflict resolution

- Flexibility

Team Roles

- Leader

- Mediator

- Motivator

- Researcher

- Time keeper

- Artist

- Other

Personality Assessment

Circle the answer that best describes you for each of the ten questions. (You may only circle one answer for each question.) When you have answered each question, total up how many questions you answered with an A, B, C and D.

1. To help recharge after a stressful day, I would prefer to:

    a) Read a book.
    b) Get together with friends.
    c) Vent to a friend or spouse.
    d) Watch television.

2. The best way to get me to do something is:

    a) Give me the reasons why I should.
    b) Explain the benefits to me.
    c) Tell me you how much you would appreciate it.
    d) Just ask.

3. I prefer to work:

    a) Alone.
    b) As a team.
    c) Whichever is less stressful.
    d) I don't care as long as I'm in charge.

4. I like to do:

    a) Puzzles & brain teasers
    b) Arts and crafts
    c) Play music
    d) Sports

5. Change is:

    a) Stressful
    b) Exciting
    c) Scary, but good
    d) Necessary

6. What is most important is:

    a) The truth
    b) Enjoyment
    c) Feelings
    d) Outcomes

7. I would describe myself as:

    a) Logical
    b) Outgoing
    c) Caring
    d) Driven

8. I am:

    a) Right
    b) Fun
    c) Loving
    d) Confident

9. Others would describe me as:

    a) Detail oriented
    b) Independent
    c) Supportive
    d) Motivated

10. I focus on:

    a) Thinking
    b) Being
    c) Feeling
    d) Doing

Scoring:

# of A's _____

# of B's _____

# of C's _____

# of D's _____

A's: Earth

B's: Wind

C's: Water

D's: Fire

Gender Communications

Men

- Compartmentalize

- Ask or Tell

- Analytical Thought

- State

- Direct

Women

- Integrate

- Hint

- Integrate Emotion

- Question

- Provide excess info

Assignment: Individual Team Member Assessment

Team member: _____

Position: _____

Personality Style: _____

Team Role: _____

What motivates me: _____

Goals:

Peek work hours: _____

How do you work best?

Individually   With a partner   In a team

Strengths:

Challenges:

Assignment: Team Assessment

How is our team diverse?

Are there any roles our team is missing? If so, is there someone who is willing and able to fill those roles?

What can we do to help motivate one another?

Do our team goals align with one another and with the company's goals?

How can the strengths of each team member best be put to use?

How can the team help support the challenges each team member faces? (Example: One team member's challenge is organization. Can other team members do things to assist that team member, such as, sending them email reminders of due dates?)

Scavenger Hunt List

Picture of a team member with…

1. A red sports car.
2. A boat.
3. An animal.
4. An employee of a fast-food restaurant.
5. With a stranger.
6. With the most interesting street sign.
7. Looking into a refrigerator (cannot be the office fridge).
8. With a body of water.
9. Wearing a hat.
10. A person wearing a costume.
11. A windmill.
12. A map.
13. An item from a restaurant with the name or logo, example TGIFridays mints.
14. A plant.
15. A vacuum cleaner. (cannot be the office vacuum cleaner)
16. A person with a beard.
17. Someone wearing flip-flops.
18. Someone wearing a uniform.
19. A couch (cannot be the couch in the office).
20. A stuffed animal.

2 LEADERSHIP

"A leader is one who knows the way, goes the way, and shows the way."

John C. Maxwell

Full Training Agenda

- ➢ **Section One: Getting Started**
  - Introduction & Biography
  - Objectives
  - Agenda
  - Icebreaker
  - Manager vs. Leader
  - Leadership Styles
  - Assignment

- ➢ **Section Two: Handling Conflict**
  - Benefits of conflict
  - Styles of handling conflict
  - Assignment
  - Communication
  - Barriers to effective listening
  - Overcoming barriers
  - Negative behaviors
  - Steps in dealing with negative behaviors
  - Additional tips
  - Assignment
  - Anger management

- ➢ **Section Three: Motivation & Change**
  - Motivating Others
  - Assignment
  - Implementing Change
  - Assignment

Manager vs. Leader

Leader

1. Promotes change
2. Utilizes conflict
3. Risk taker
4. Passionate
5. Has and shares a vision

Manager

1. Implements change when necessary, otherwise happy with status quo
2. Avoids conflict
3. Risk minimizer
4. Controlling
5. Follows and implements objectives

Leadership Styles

1. Autocratic/Transactional/Authoritarian

2. Bureaucratic/ Paternalistic

3. Democratic/Participative/ Transformational

4. Laissez-Faire

Assignment: Leadership

Complete a basic assessment to help determine which style of leadership would be the best fit for your team.

1. How would you describe the company culture?

2. What are the strengths and weaknesses of the teams?

3. What are the individual team member's strengths and weaknesses?

4. What is the current style of leadership that is being utilized?

5. What is working about the current style of leadership?

6. What is not working about the current style of leadership?

7. What benefits could come from the use of each style of leadership?

    a. Autocratic/Transactional/Authoritarian

    b. Bureaucratic/ Paternalistic

    c. Democratic/Participative/ Transformational

    d. Laissez-Faire

8. What would be the drawbacks of using each style of leadership?

    a. Autocratic/Transactional/Authoritarian

    b. Bureaucratic/ Paternalistic

    c. Democratic/Participative/ Transformational

    d. Laissez-Faire

9. What are the company goals?

10. How could using each style of leadership help us to reach our goals?

    a. Autocratic/Transactional/Authoritarian

    b. Bureaucratic/ Paternalistic

    c. Democratic/Participative/ Transformational

    d. Laissez-Faire

11. Would using any of the styles of leadership deter us from reaching our goals? How?

    a. Autocratic/Transactional/Authoritarian

    b. Bureaucratic/ Paternalistic

    c. Democratic/Participative/ Transformational

    d. Laissez-Faire

12. Are we willing and able to take the time required to implement the style of leadership we desire?

13. What changes would need to be made to implement each style of leadership?

    a. Autocratic/Transactional/Authoritarian

    b. Bureaucratic/ Paternalistic

    c. Democratic/Participative/ Transformational

    d. Laissez-Faire

14. After assessment, I believe the best style of leadership for our team/company would be:

Because:

15. I believe the company/our team could benefit from utilizing this style of leadership in the following ways:

16. Implementing this style of leadership would require the following:

The Five Styles of Dealing with Conflict

1. Avoidance

2. Accommodation

3. Compromise

4. Collaboration

5. Competition

Assignment: Conflict Resolution

Use a personal example of a conflict that your team has faced. Determine which style of conflict resolution was used. Then analyze the possible outcome with both positive and negative effects of how the conflict may have been handled using each of the other styles of conflict resolution. Which option would have been the best way to handle the conflict?

Conflict:

Conflict resolution style used:

Outcome:

Using the Avoidance style of conflict resolution:

Using the Accommodation style of conflict resolution:

Using the Compromise style of conflict resolution:

Using the Collaboration style of conflict resolution:

Using the Competition style of conflict resolution:

Best option for handling this type of conflict:

Why:

Problem Solving

• What would make the situation better?

• What are possible solutions?

• How can this be resolved?

• What can others do to help resolve the issue?

Handling Negative Behaviors

1. Have clearly stated policies on company culture, expectations and values.

2. Provide company training for all employees.

3. Lead by example.

4. Arrange a one-on-one meeting to get to discuss the behavior and get to the root of the issue. Keep records of meetings.

5. If the behavior continues, conduct one-on-one coaching to change the behavior. Keep records of meetings.

6. If the behavior persists, take disciplinary action.

Assignment: Handling Negative Behaviors

Use an example of a negative behavior you have had to handle. Utilize the steps for handling negative behaviors to create a simulated report on how you would handle the situation using this model.

1. Behavior:

2. Company's policy regarding this behavior:

3. Trainings employee has received regarding this behavior:

4. Have I modeled the appropriate alternative to this behavior?

    a. Example of how appropriate behavior has been modeled:

5. Arrange a one-on-one meeting to discuss the behavior and get to the root of the problem.

    a. Do they understand why you are meeting with them?

    b. Are they aware of the company's policies regarding this behavior?
    c. What reasons do they give for the behavior?
    d. Explanation given of the impact their actions have/may have on the team.

6. Possible solutions for adjusting the behavior:

7. Begin to focus on solutions.

8. Keep records of the meeting.

    a. Date:
    b. Time:
    c. Persons involved.

    d. What was discussed:

    e. Plan for moving forward:

    f. One-on-one coaching to be conducted on:

9. Keep records of the meeting.

    a. Dates:
    b. Times:
    c. Persons involved:

    d. What was discussed or what training was conducted:

    e. Plan for moving forward:

    f. Copies of any training materials they completed.

10. Disciplinary action required:

Motivation

Level One: Physiological needs

Level Two: Safety

Level Three: Social Needs

Level Four: Esteem

Level Five: Self-actualization

Assignment: Motivation

Provide each of your team members with a copy of the list on the following page to conduct a survey of employee motivation to familiarize yourself with the team's preferences.

Follow by making a list of ideas on how to motivate staff at each level.

Level one: Physiological needs

Level two: Safety

Level Three: Social

Level Four: Esteem

Level Five: Self-Actualization

Rate the following from 1-15 according to preference.

1 being greatest desire, 15 being the least important.

_____Caring for/supporting others

_____Career development/success

_____Fun/recreation

_____Comfort/relaxation

_____Influence/leadership

_____Health/balance/energy

_____Learning/knowledge/discovery

_____Materials/possessions

_____Security/money

_____Recognition/praise

_____Social/popularity/acceptance

_____Prestige/status/reputation

_____Teaching/coaching others

_____Task accomplishment/achievement/problem solving

_____Other _____

Assignment: Implementing Change

Generate an idea for a possible change. Develop a plan for implementing the change, based on the step by step process.

Step One: Create a Team

What are the strengths of each individual on the team?

- Who are the experts in each area?

- Who has the *"ear of the masses"*?

- Who can act as a mentor?

- Who is opposed to the change?

- Who is responsible for the budget?

- Who can best gather information to help tailor the process?

- Who can work in pilot project, then as a mentor?

- Other areas of strength to be utilized.

What role/responsibility will each team member take on?

- Leader

- Task manager

- Details – strategies

- Public relations

- Risk management

- Mentor

- Trainer

- Designer

- Assessment Director

- Other Roles

Step Two: Align the Team

• What are our reasons for wanting/needing change?

• What are the goals? (short and long term)

• Vision statement regarding this change.

• How are things currently done? /What is the current process?

• What is working and what is not?

• Who all/what all will be affected by this change?

• What tools will this change require?

• What are the risks?

• What is the current attitude/atmosphere?

• Will change be accepted well?

• What will help to motivate change?

Step Three: Develop a Change Plan

- Brainstorm, gathering ideas (be sure to utilize the ideas and suggestions of all team members).

- Research.

- Determine the pros/cons of each idea.

- Consider the possible effects on employees, stakeholders and customers.

- Consider what possible issues may arise, what the causes would be and possible solutions.

- What tools and resources will the change require?

SWOT Analysis:

Strengths: Internal positive factors

What do we do well?

What resources do we have?

What competitive advantage do we have over our competitors?

Weaknesses: Internal negative factors (these can be fixed)

Where can we make improvements?

What do we need to do/offer to beat our competitors?

What resources are we lacking?

Do we have the experts we need on staff?

Do we have the technology we need?

Are we in a good location?

Opportunities: External positive factors

What opportunities are in the market or environment that we could take advantage of?

Do others view our business in a positive way?

Are there any new trends in the market that create an opportunity for us?

Is it a short term fad?

Do we need to move quickly or with caution?

Threats: External negative factors

Who are our competitors?

What factors, beyond our control, may we be at risk for?

Has there been any significant changes in our costs?

Are there any shifts in the economy, government regulations or consumer behavior that would affect us?

Are there new products or services that make us obsolete?

Step Four: Implementation

Approaches to implementing new processes

Typical Approach

Fast Approach

Careful Approach

Distributed Approach

Development Approach

Which implementation approached will be utilized?

Step Five: Training

What type of training is required?

Dates and times for training:

Who will develop each training?

Who will facilitate each training?

Who will participate in each training?

What materials are needed for each training?

Step Six: Evaluation

What do you like about the new process?

What do you dislike about the new process?

What suggestions do you have for improving on this process?

How have things improved since the new process was implemented?

Has anything been more challenging since the new process? If so, what and how?

Other questions to ask regarding the change and/or specifics of it.

Ideas for celebrating successes.

Wee Communicate, LLC. Objective Comprehension Worksheet

1. What is one difference between a manager and a leader?

2. Name two styles of leadership.
    1.

    2.
3. Explain one of the benefit of conflict.

4. List two styles of handling conflict.
    1.

    2.

5. List two barriers to effective listening and how to overcome them.
    1.

    2.

6. Define SWOT analysis.

7. List three of the levels of motivation.
    1.

    2.

    3.

Certificate of Completion

This certifies that

_____

has successfully completed

Leadership Training for

_____

On _____, 20_____

Participant Signature_____

Facilitator Signature_____

Wee Communicate, LLC. Training Feedback Form

To what extent was the training useful/helpful?

Not useful at all = 1   Very useful = 10

1   2   3   4   5   6   7   8   9   10

Please share two things you have learned from the training that you believe will be beneficial to you in your position.

1.

2.

What part of the training was most useful for you and why?

What part of the training was the least useful for you and why? If you have suggestions for improvement please share in the space provided below.

Did you enjoy spending time in the training?

I did not enjoy it at all = 1

I so enjoyed it that I am excited for the next training = 10

1   2   3   4   5   6   7   8   9   10

I would not recommend this training = 1
I would highly recommend this training = 10

1   2   3   4   5   6   7   8   9   10

Additional comments:

3 DIVERSITY

"No two people are exactly alike, therefore, anyone who is not you is diverse from you."

Caroline Wee

Full Training Agenda

➤ **Section One: Getting Started**
- Introduction & Biography
- Objectives
- Set the stage
- Agenda
- Icebreaker
- Defining Diversity
- Related Terms and Concepts
- Transition/Review

➤ **Section Two: How are we diverse?**
- How are we diverse?
- Stereotypes about diversity
- Is that a fact?
- Activity: Is that a fact?
- Benefits of diversity
- Activity: People Bingo
- Transition/Review

➤ **Section Three: Barriers**
- What are the barriers?
- Overcoming barriers
- Communication
- Lack of…
- Resistance to Change
- Activity: Walk a mile in someone else's shoes
- Transition/Review

➤ **Section Four: Encouraging Diversity**
- Personally
- As an organization
- Activity: My favorite thing about you
- Transition/Review

➢ **Section Five: Managing Diversity Conflicts**
  • Managing Diversity Conflict
  • Scenarios
  • What to do if you have been discriminated against
  • Moving Forward
  • Review

Training Expectations

- Participants should come to each training session on time, with an open-mind and positive attitude.

- This is a safe, non-judgmental space. Topics discussed in this training are not to be discussed or held against other participants outside of this training.

- Participants should feel free to speak openly and honestly, but also respectfully and compassionately.

- Participants should take turns speaking and limit side conversations. Participants should remain patient and respectful when others are speaking. The facilitator will assist in keeping participants on track.

- Disrespectful, threatening, derogatory or degrading comments will not be permitted.

- Questions or concerns should be discussed with the facilitator.

- Be open to the positive experience and opportunity this training and our time together have to offer.

Stereotypes

Age

- I'm young, so I must be lazy.
- I'm retired, so I must be slow and bad at technology.

Race/Ethnicity

- I'm Asian so I must be good at math.
- I'm African American so I must be good at sports.

Socioeconomic status

- I'm on assistance, so I must be lazy.

Gender

- I'm a woman, so I must like to cook.
- I'm a man, so I must like sports.

Religion

- I'm Christian, so I must hate homosexuals.
- I'm an atheist, so I must be evil and have no morals.

Political views

- I'm a Republican, so I must be a religious fundamentalist nut.
- I'm a Democrat, so I must be an environmentalist or atheist.

Sexual Orientation

- I hang out with gays, so I must be gay too.
- I'm into theater and art, so I must be a homosexual.

Physical/Mental abilities

- I'm skinny, so I must be anorexic.
- I'm a blonde, so I must be stupid.

Personality/Learning Styles

- I'm outgoing, so I must be ditzy.
- I need to have things read to me, so I must be unintelligent.

Educational & Work Background

- I do physical labor, so I must not be educated.
- I am a manager, so I must be arrogant.

Geographic Location & Culture

- I'm from the south, so I must be stupid.
- I'm from the north, so I must like to hunt.

Marital & Parental Status

- I'm a parent, so I must not have any other priorities.
- I am single, so I must have a lot of free time.

Is That A Fact?

1. China has the largest population in the world.

2. Boys are better at sports than girls.

3. Kimchi is a popular food in South Korea.

4. French people are rude.

5. African Americans are better at sports.

6. The Nile is the longest river in the world.

7. Older employees are slower learners.

8. People who do not have children have more free-time.

9. Women perform 66% of the worlds' work, but receive only 11% of the world's income.

10. Homeless people are lazy.

11. Homosexuality and same-sex couplings have been honored in ancient India and Greece.

12. People who are dyslexic are unintelligent.

13. People who are kinesthetic learners, enjoy working with their hands.

14. People who are not married have "loose" morals.

15. This is the best organization to work for.

Personal Diversity Assessment

On a scale of 1 to 5 rate how strongly you agree with the following statements. 1= low 5 = high

1. I appreciate those who are different than myself.

2. I avoid telling jokes that others may find offensive.

3. I never make remarks that "push buttons". Example: remarks about race, political views, religion, gender etc.

4. I listen when communicating and do not interrupt others.

5. I check my assumptions (fact or opinion) about others who are different than myself.

6. I take into consideration the effect of diverse views, beliefs and opinions in communicating with others.

7. When experiencing frustration or conflict I take time to assess the situation, i.e. the feelings, beliefs, and views of others.

8. I realize others may stereotype me, and I try to overcome any incorrect assumptions they may make about me.

9. I do not judge people on their accent or language fluency.

10. I recognize I am a product of my own upbringing, and my way is not the only way.

11. I am patient and flexible. I can accept different ways of getting a job done as long as the results are good.

12. I welcome creativity, variety and change.

13. I am interested in people who are different than myself and seek out opportunities for learning things about people who are different than myself.

14. I listen carefully.

15. I am an effective communicator.

16. I like people and accept them as they are.

17. I am sensitive to the feelings of others, I observe their reaction and adjust accordingly.

18. I am aware of my prejudices and consciously try to control my assumptions about others.

19. I ask for clarification when I don't understand someone or something.

20. I recognize my personal values and know which values I am able to compromise without losing my integrity.

0-50 You most likely experience difficulty working in a diverse setting and could benefit from further training.

50-80 You are headed in the right direction, but there is room for improvement.

80+ You value diversity and are able to work well in a diverse environment.

Organizational Diversity Assessment

1. Does your organization, company, or agency have a specific commitment or contract to serve all forms of diverse groups?

   Describe:

2. Does your organization, company, or agency reflect the diverse community and consumer population it serves?

   How or how not?

3. Does your organization, company, or agency utilize the skills, knowledge and talents of its diverse staff?

4. Does your organization, company, or agency have the ability to accommodate:

   People in wheelchairs or walkers: _____

   People who are blind: _____

   People who are deaf: _____

   People with a learning disability: _____

   Variety of personalities: _____

   Variety of learning styles: _____

   English as a 2nd language: _____

5. Would you consider your organization, company, or agency to be diverse in regard to:

    Age: _____

    Gender: _____

    Race/Ethnicity: _____

    Educational/Work Background: _____

    Religion: _____

    Sexual Orientation: _____

    Socioeconomic status: _____

    Physical/Mental abilities: _____

    Military experience: _____

    Marital & Parental status: _____

6. Does your organization, company, or agency represent diversity at each level of position and wages?

7. Does your company have a plan in place for handling diversity conflicts or complaints?

8. Does your organization, company, or agency incorporate the special concerns and needs of diverse populations' cultural healing practices, celebration of cultural holidays, discussion groups on race and/or culture in relation to behavior, etc.?

9. Does your organization, company, or agency promote equality in regard to:

      Age: _____

      Gender: _____

      Race/Ethnicity: _____

      Educational/Work Background: _____

      Religion: _____

      Sexual Orientation: _____

      Socioeconomic status: _____

      Physical/Mental abilities: _____

      Military experience: _____

      Marital & Parental status: _____

10. Have you ever been discriminated against?

    Describe:

11. Do you consider your organization, company, or agency to be aware and sensitive to the diverse needs of others?

Diversity Action Plan

Diversity Mission Statement

Diversity Goal

Outcomes

Outcome One:

Strategic action steps:

Outcome Two:

Strategic action steps:

Outcome Three:

Strategic action steps:

Methods for assessment of the Diversity Action Plan

Commitment to Diversity

I _____acknowledge receipt of
_____'s Diversity Action Plan. I have read and understand the expectations of the plan. I understand that by signing this form I am stating my intention and commitment to the encouragement and promotion of the Diversity Action Plan.

Managing Conflicts of Diversity

Scenario 1

There is obvious tension between two employees.

Scenario 2

One employee displays PETA (People for the Ethical Treatment of Animals) information & posters in their cubicle, another displays pro-hunting information & posters.

Scenario 3

Someone says that they are having a softball game on Sunday, but they know Susan won't want to come. Susan feels that it was said because she is overweight. The other employee says that they knew she couldn't go because she has church functions and they go to the same church.

Scenario 4

Inappropriate conversations and/or jokes are being discussed.

What to do if you have been Discriminated Against

- Write it down immediately. Be specific.

- Include:

  o Date
  o Time
  o Location
  o What persons were involved
  o What persons (if any) were witness to the discrimination
  o What exactly was said/done

- Follow your organizations policies for reporting.
- Know who to go to in your organization.

Wee Communicate, LLC. Objective Comprehension Worksheet Sample

1. How do you define diversity?
2. What do you do if you have been a victim of discrimination?
3. List four ways in which our organization is diverse.
    1.
    2.
    3.
    4.
4. List two barriers to diversity.
    1.
    2.
5. List four ways to overcome the barriers to diversity.
    1.
    2.
    3.
    4.
6. List two of the benefits of diversity
    1.
    2.

Certificate of Completion

This certifies that

_____

has successfully completed

Diversity Training for

_____

On _____, 20_____

Participant Signature_____

Facilitator Signature_____

Wee Communicate, LLC. Training Feedback Form Sample

To what extent was the training useful/helpful?

Not useful at all = 1   Very useful = 10

1   2   3   4   5   6   7   8   9   10

Please share two things you have learned from the training that you believe will be beneficial to you in your position.

1.

2.

What part of the training was most useful for you and why?

What part of the training was the least useful for you and why? If you have suggestions for improvement please share in the space provided below.

Did you enjoy spending time in the training?

I did not enjoy it at all = 1

I so enjoyed it that I am excited for the next training = 10

1   2   3   4   5   6   7   8   9   10

I would not recommend this training = 1
I would highly recommend this training = 10

1   2   3   4   5   6   7   8   9   10

Additional comments:

4 SEXUAL HARASSMENT

"If your flirting strategy is indistinguishable from harassment, it's not everyone else that's the problem." ~ John Scalzi

Full Training Agenda

➢ **Section One: Getting Started**
- Introduction & Biography
- Set the stage
- Objectives
- Agenda
- Icebreaker
- Defining Sexual Harassment
- Who
- Types of Sexual Harassment
- Activity: Sort Which Sort
- Review

➢ **Section Two : Regulation**
- Effects of Sexual Harassment
- The Law
- Liability
- Prevention
- Company Policy
- Review

➢ **Section Three: What to do**
- Company Policies
- Complaint Procedures
- Investigation
- Review

➢ **Section Four: Information**
- Flirting and Dating versus Harassment
- How to Handle Unwanted Attention
- Reporting
- Review

Training Expectations

- Participants should come to each training session on time, with an open-mind and positive attitude.
- This is a safe, non-judgmental space. Topics discussed in this training are not to be discussed or held against other participants outside of this training.
- Participants should feel free to speak openly and honestly, but also respectfully and compassionately.
- Participants should take turns speaking and limit side conversations.
- Participants should remain patient and respectful when others are speaking. The facilitator will assist in keeping participants on track.
- Disrespectful, threatening, derogatory or degrading comments will not be permitted.
- Questions or concerns should be discussed with the facilitator.
- Be open to the positive experience and opportunity this training and our time together have to offer.

Categories of Sexual Harassment

Category One: Quid Pro Quo "Something for something".

Examples:

- An employee is offered increased wages in return for sexual intercourse.
- An employee is told they may keep their job if they agree to go on a date with their supervisor.
- Professional opportunities are withheld from an employee as a means to punish for refusal or require submission of sexual conduct.

Category Two: Hostile Environment: Behaviors that can constitute a hostile environment under the law include, but are not limited to: offensive remarks, leering, inappropriate or unwelcome physical contact, sexual posters and sexual jokes or comments of a sexual nature. Typically an isolated incident is not considered hostile environment harassment unless it extraordinarily flagrant or outrageous or alters an employee's terms or conditions of employment.

Activity: Sort Which Sort

1. An employee has a sexually explicit calendar hanging in their office.

2. A manager asks an employee on a date. The employee does not accept the invitation. The employee receives all low marks on their performance review, even though they are leading their department in productivity.

3. An employee overhears another employee telling a sexist joke to a friend on the phone.

4. An employee feels that their supervisor is always trying to find an excuse to touch them in some way.

5. Every day in the employee lounge, an employee discusses their activities of a sexual nature.

6. An employee makes unwanted sexual advances toward another employee. The employee states that they will recommend the other employee to the supervisor for an opening in management.

7. An employee is sending email jokes of a sexual nature.

Sexual Harassment Policy (Sample)

Table of Contents

1. Sexual Harassment Policy Statement
2. Definitions
3. Examples
4. Grievance Procedures
5. Non-retaliation
6. Disciplinary Action
7. For more information

Sexual Harassment Policy Statement

It is the policy of this company to provide an environment free from sexual harassment. Any actions that may be considered as sexual harassment will not be tolerated.

Definitions

The EEOC (Equal Employment Opportunity Commission) defines sexual harassment as:

"Unwelcome sexual advances, requests for sexual favors, and other verbal or physical conduct of a sexual nature constitute sexual harassment when:

- Submission to such conduct is made either explicitly or implicitly a term or condition of an individual's employment,
- Submission to or rejection of such conduct by an individual is used as the basis for employment decisions affecting such individuals, or
- Such conduct has the purpose or effect of unreasonably interfering with an individual's work performance or creating an intimidating, hostile, or offensive working environment."

Examples

Verbal:

- Comments about a person's body or sex life.
- Propositions or pressures for sexual favors or to engage in sexual activity.
- Sexual remarks.
- Jokes based on race, gender, age, disability, sexual orientation, religion, etc....
- Insults or innuendoes based on race, gender, age, disability, sexual orientation, religion, etc....
- Whistling.
- "Cat calls" or referring to someone as a: stud, hunk, babe and etc....

Non-Verbal:

- Gestures
- Staring
- Touching
- Hugging
- Patting
- Blocking a person's movement
- Standing too close
- Brushing against a person's body
  Display of offensive materials that are, sexually suggestive, racist, derogatory or degrading such as: photos, calendars, pictures, cartoons or drawings.

Grievance Procedures

- If an employee believes they are being harassed, they should notify their supervisor as soon as possible.

- Anyone who becomes aware of harassment should notify their supervisor as soon as possible.

- Any client who believes they are being harassed by an employee should ask to speak to a supervisor immediately.

- Any employee who believes they are being harassed by a client should notify their supervisor immediately.

- If an employee is uncomfortable discussing the harassment with their supervisor, they should contact _____ in the Human Resources Department as soon as possible.

- It is the responsibility of the company to investigate and take reasonable action on reports of sexual harassment. If the company does not promptly respond to any report of sexual harassment, it is the right of the complainant to file a state or federal harassment complaint. More information can be found on the EEOC website at http://www.eeoc.gov

- Upon notification of a harassment complaint, the company will promptly begin an impartial and confidential investigation.

- Investigation will include direct interviews with the complainant, the accused, witnesses and anyone having information relating to the complaint. The parties of the complaint will be notified after the investigation of the findings, their options and any ramifications related to them.

Non-retaliation

The company expressly prohibits any kind of retaliation against anyone reporting or assisting in the investigation of a harassment complaint.

Disciplinary Action

Disciplinary or corrective action will be incurred by anyone who engages in actions of sexual harassment, retaliation against anyone reporting harassment, retaliation against anyone involved in an investigation or anyone involved in misconduct such as violating the confidentiality of an investigation, providing false information or false accusations.

Disciplinary action may include one or more of the following:

- Written reprimand.
- Suspension without pay.
- Mandatory training or counseling on sexual harassment.
- Reassignment.
- Demotion.
- Discharge from the company.

For more information contact:

- The Human Resources Department
- Department of Workforce Development Equal Rights Division
- Civil Rights Bureau
- EEOC (Equal Employment Opportunity Commission)

I _____, do state that I have read and understand the sexual harassment policy of _____. I hereby agree to adhere to the company's zero tolerance policy for a non-retaliation and sexual harassment free environment.

Signed _____Date_____

Sexual Harassment Interview: Complaint Form

Company Name: _____

Date: _____

Investigator Name: _____

Complainant Name: _____

Complainant Title/Position: _____

Alleged Harasser Name: _____

Alleged Harasser Title/Position: _____

Name and Title/Position of witness(es): _____

_____

_____

When did the harassment take place?

Date: _____

Time: _____

Where did the harassment take place? (Specific location – room, email, etc....)

What specifically was said and/or done?

What, if anything, did you do or say in response?

Did you tell anyone else? If so, who did you tell and what did you say? All conversations about the alleged harassment will remain confidential and will be discussed on a 'need to know' basis.

List any injuries or adverse consequences of the harassment (example medical, missed work, missed promotion, etc....)

List of evidence to submit

Attach copies of evidence (example: copies of harassing emails, pictures of graffiti, etc....)

Signature of investigator _____

Date _____

Signature of complainant _____

Date _____

Sexual Harassment Interview: Accused

Company Name: _____

Date: _____

Investigator Name: _____

Accused Name: _____

Accused Title/Position: _____

Complainant Name: Not presented

Date the alleged harassment took place: _____

Time the alleged harassment took place: _____

Description of alleged harassment:

What is the accused's response to the allegations?

If the accused does not agree with the allegations, what is their interpretation of what took place during that time?

If the accused does not agree with the allegations, why do they feel someone accused them of this allegation?

Do you know of anyone else that may have relevant information? If so, who and what information would they have?

All conversations about the alleged harassment will remain confidential and will be discussed on a 'need to know' basis.

Signature of investigator _____

Date _____

Signature of complainant _____

Date _____

Sexual Harassment Interview: Witness Form

Company Name: _____

Date: _____

Investigator Name: _____

Witness Name: _____

Witness Title/Position: _____

Complainant Name: Not presented

Alleged Harasser Name: Not presented

When did the harassment take place?

Date: _____

Time: _____

Where did the harassment take place? (Specific location – room, email, etc....)

Witnesses' description of alleged harassment:

What, if anything, did you do or say in response?

Did you tell anyone else? If so, who did you tell and what did you say?

All conversations about the alleged harassment will remain confidential and will be discussed on a 'need to know' basis.

Signature of investigator _____

Date _____

Signature of witness _____

Date _____

Wee Communicate, LLC. Objective Comprehension Worksheet Sample

1. How do you define sexual harassment?

2. What do you do if you have been a victim of harassment?

3. List the two types of sexual harassment.

    1.

    2.

4. List four effects of sexual harassment.

    1.

    2.

    3.

    4.

5. Describe the company's policy on sexual harassment.

6. Explain the difference between flirting and harassment.

Certificate of Completion

This certifies that

_____

has successfully completed

Sexual Harassment Training for

_____

On _____, 20_____

Participant Signature_____

Facilitator Signature_____

Wee Communicate, LLC. Training Feedback Form Sample

To what extent was the training useful/helpful?

Not useful at all = 1   Very useful = 10

1   2   3   4   5   6   7   8   9   10

Please share two things you have learned from the training that you believe will be beneficial to you in your position.

1.
2.

What part of the training was most useful for you and why?

What part of the training was the least useful for you and why? If you have suggestions for improvement please share in the space provided below.

Did you enjoy spending time in the training?

I did not enjoy it at all = 1

I so enjoyed it that I am excited for the next training = 10

1   2   3   4   5   6   7   8   9   10

I would not recommend this training = 1
I would highly recommend this training = 10

1   2   3   4   5   6   7   8   9   10

Additional comments:

ABOUT THE AUTHOR

Caroline Wee enjoys life's journey and is always ready for an adventure. At 19, she left the Midwest to experience the metropolitan life in New York City. During her two years on the East Coast, Caroline became even more interested in diversity, culture, and organizational differences. Upon returning to the Midwest, Caroline received her Bachelor of Arts in Organizational Communications from the University of Wisconsin-Eau Claire. Her first job after graduating was spending one year in South Korea teaching English to students.

When she returned to the United States after her South Korean adventure, Caroline worked at a university as an admissions representative, presenting college opportunities to high school students. When budget cuts eliminated her position with the university, Caroline decided to pursue her dream. Gathering all her strengths and experiences together, Caroline created Wee Communicate, an organization that provides training and motivational speaking. By utilizing her core competencies of building rapport with diverse groups of people, her desire is to bring out the best in everyone.

As an experienced trainer and speaker, Caroline brings her passion and enthusiasm to all of her clients. Caroline firmly believes in 'walking the talk' and consistently states that she would never ask you to do something that she has not or would not do herself. Her expectations of others and herself are real; she knows that no one is perfect, including herself. By owning who we are and pushing to become a better self, Caroline believes we can make a difference within ourselves and in the world. She lives her life by the words of Nelson Mandela: "Education is the most powerful weapon which you can use to change the world." Her favorite quote is from Sheldon Cooper: "What's life without whimsy?" Caroline combines these two ideals to educate and entertain her audiences. For more information about Caroline and Wee Communicate Trainings visit www.weecommunicate.com

www.ingramcontent.com/pod-product-compliance
Lightning Source LLC
Chambersburg PA
CBHW080559180526
45168CB00007B/2716